Author

Ann-Marie McMahon is a graduate of University College Dublin and a registered psychologist.

She is Director of Aftercare at St John of God Hospital, Stillorgan, County Dublin, where her particular interests include counselling and psychotherapy.

She has a degree in Economics and Public Relations and has worked in these related areas, as well as in personnel management.

She conducts Personal Development, Human Relations and Communication courses for the Community and Adult Education Centre at St Patrick's College, Maynooth.

Joanne McElgunn graduated from the College of Commerce, Rathmines, Dublin, and is now working as a freelance journalist with national newspapers.

GU00706131

ISSUES NOT TISSUES

A fresh approach to Personal Development

Issues not Tissues

A FRESH APPROACH TO PERSONAL
DEVELOPMENT

Ann-Marie McMahon

with

Joanne McElgunn

Illustrations by

Alan Corsini

MOYTURA PRESS

DUBLIN

This book was typeset by
Gilbert Gough Typesetting for
Moytura Press,
4 Arran Quay, Dublin 7.

BRITISH LIBRARY CATALOGUING IN PUBLICATION DATA
A CIP Catalogue record for this book is available from the British
Library.

ISBN 1-871305-11-X

Printed in Ireland by
Colour Books Ltd.

Contents

Dedication

This book is dedicated to everyone who has passed through my life and in some way influenced me to put my thoughts into writing.

Acknowledgement

This book was written with the assistance of Joanne McIlgunn. Her enthusiasm, never ending sense of fun and excitement for living created an atmosphere for us both to enjoy the experience of writing *Issues not Tissues*.

Joanne had the ability to put my thoughts into words. Her journalistic skills made it all possible. Thank you, Joanne. I enjoyed your company — and thanks also, to your flatmates for putting up with us on those long winter evenings.

I must say a particular word of thanks to Alan Corsini, illustrator par excellence, whose illustrations enliven the text so admirably.

I would especially like to thank my publisher, Gerard O'Connor, who initially stirred the embers and wafted the creative flame. Gerry's team put it all into action and in particular Karen McGrath.

I would also like to thank Janet Brown for her editing — it was a pleasure to work with someone who put so much effort and enthusiasm into such a short amount of time.

Finally, thank you to my family and friends and colleagues in St John of God's Hospital who have supported me in my life and career. This book is ultimately about support and friendship.

Foreword

How I live my life is the real 'issue' — not how others decide I should. Very often, none of us want to face up to life's real issues. We spend our time ducking the issue by avoiding reality, confrontation and the resulting responsibility.

We use such gadgets as masks, labels, phoney language and defence mechanisms as props for the play of life. But, remember, life is not a dress rehearsal. Every day we play the leading role in our own production. But, some people believe this play is about fantasy, reliving old reels and projecting into a futuristic film.

We can create issues to side-step an important decision; to keep people at bay and avoid the challenge of living. Life can be painful and who likes pain? But, with recovery, the pain diminishes and there is room to grow.

Personal growth comes after a lot of searching and a smattering of ups and downs. We can gain the ability to challenge ourselves and allow ourselves the freedom to change.

Each individual grows at his or her own pace. There is no right or wrong answer to the way to go about this. Grab the opportunities as they arise, but also be ready to hold onto them.

Too often, we make 'issues' out of things that don't concern us. We grope in the dark and lose our bearings. Time and energy is wasted. We can end up emotionally drained, flooded by negative thoughts and scraping the bottom of our 'self-esteem' barrel.

The resulting tears of pain and frustration has us reaching for the tissues.

CHAPTER 1

My Photograph

"Put that camera away!" When somebody tries to take your photograph, do you ever find yourself using these words. The automatic cry can signal a deeper response inside many of us. Why is it when you flick through photographs of yourself that you sometimes cringe with embarrassment?

What do you expect? Perfection? Yet you know, inside, that you can never achieve this. But perhaps you could feel more satisfied with your photographs after a bit of self scrutiny. The camera may never lie, but many of us refuse to see the truth.

If you can open the pages of your mental album what images come to mind? Are they black and white or brightly coloured? Are they static or filled with action? Are they solitary, or are you surrounded by friends? At what age has your mental camera captured you? Are the pictures all out of date? Are there gaps where no photographs exist?

Do your photographs help define how you thought and felt at a particular time? Maybe you were sad, but you struck a happy pose. Perhaps there was someone special by your side and they're not around now. Perhaps the photograph has lost its gloss, or has faded with time.

Flicking through your collection of mental photographs can tell many tales. Photographs sometimes reveal more than the external image. How often has the camera's lens caught you unexpectedly, revealing that part of you you were trying to hide?

1

Photographs can help you remember what made you sad or happy. They can trigger memories, some perhaps you would rather forget. They can show you at your best and at your worst.

The chances are that you have pushed some of your mental photographs to the back of the album. You have hidden them away, hoping that you will forget their very existence. It could be that the photographs are too painful to examine. Maybe you were at your lowest ebb. Perhaps the picture was taken during a time of mourning. Maybe a particular picture makes you feel guilty and anxious, and looking at it now makes you feel vulnerable and exposed.

Looking at your mental photographs also forces you to make certain decisions. You can take stock of changes and examine whether these changes came about through self effort, conditioning or peer pressure. You can also decide to let someone else examine your photographs and talk you through the good and bad times.

MY SELF ESTEEM

Many people are not aware of their own self worth. When you look at your picture you feel apprehensive, but you don't know why. Often, this is because the value you place on yourself changes at different times. For instance, if your present circumstances are good, your self esteem is high and you can laugh off those crazy photos. But if your spirits are low, no matter how good the photograph is, you cannot see its good qualities.

If you look beyond the visual image in your albums you realise the way you were thinking, feeling and even behaving. Very often how people behave is a reflection of how they feel about themselves. Some people cope well, recognising faults, failures and limitations. Others never realise their potential because they spend their time seeking approval from everyone else, losing themselves in the process.

Approval-seeking behaviour stems from not being able to give yourself permission to make a mistake or to make a statement about yourself. Perhaps no-one ever endorsed your efforts or abilities, so you always felt you had to seek other people's reactions to your decisions. Approval-seeking behaviour can be exhausting and time wasting. The only way to get out of this familiar limbo is to start revaluing yourself and recognising that what you say and do is as valuable as anyone else.

SELF APPROVAL

Let's take an example of this type of behaviour. You've purchased a garment, brought it home, and removed the tags. You put it on and model it in front of the mirror. However, the mirror cannot tell you what you really want to hear: "You look stunning". And you're unable to say it to yourself. So, you begin seeking approval from others by asking whether you look good and whether you made a worthwhile purchase.

Likewise, you may use this scenario in other situations where you feel unable to give yourself a well deserved pat on the back. Somehow you still want to be that little child who sought praise from his or her parents in order to be approved, stimulated and confident. In adult life, you should be able to approve yourself, but unfortunately this is not always the case, because often you are left with a residue of approval-seeking feelings.

Approval or attention-seeking behaviour can become a life-time companion, never allowing you the freedom to justify your own choices. Basically, you cannot stand on your own two feet. You depend on others to provide the props.

REDESIGNING YOUR OWN PICTURE

First of all you must become aware of how you behave and react in various situations. Ask yourself the question, "Am I comfortable with what I am doing and am I getting a positive feedback?" Do you like what is going on around you? Do you feel controlled by the situation rather than in control of your own actions?

If you are not comfortable you can always look at other options. Maybe you need to acquire certain skills, or perhaps you need support to assist you along the way. If your mental picture is not meeting your needs, perhaps you could examine the following:

1. Self awareness: where are you now and where do you want to be?

2. Self acceptance: how comfortable are you about yourself and your circumstances?

3. Self exploration: what image do you have of yourself and do you want to change this?

4. Self approval: do you affirm yourself and your own choices?

Does your new photograph meet your needs? Do you want to change yourself or maintain what you have got? Perhaps the following chapters in this book will help you reframe the image of yourself and assist you to achieve this image — even give it a gilt edge.

CHAPTER TWO

Feelings

Our feelings about ourselves nestle inside as an integral part of our emotional system. They are always sending us messages, yet we often find it difficult to understand them, and even ignore them. Feelings protect us from danger by warning us that something is wrong. Feelings, when they are working correctly, look after our best interests and we should make a special effort to listen to them and become acquainted with them. If you choose to ignore your feelings you end up living inside your head and losing touch with what is going on inside you, and between yourself and others. This may result in you using feelings inappropriately.

Feelings are universal. They are the one common language through which people communicate. Your tears, joy, sadness and anger will be recognised anywhere in the world. You can send out messages without ever opening your mouth. However, although we all share the same feelings, we don't all experience the same feelings at the same time. This can give rise to conflict. You have to learn how to identify and label your feelings. In naming them you can lay claim to owning them.

Feelings are like property which you have a responsibility towards. You must make decisions on how to look after and control your feelings. Many people find this an awesome task, because it is very often much easier to place the responsibility on someone else when the feeling is uncomfortable.

Imagine being in a supermarket where the labels have all been removed from the produce. You take a chance, choose some items, not knowing whether they are the ones you want. When you get home you realise the futility of your shopping trip. Likewise, not labelling your feelings correctly can be futile. Take someone who is experiencing extreme sadness and perhaps a sense of loss. Instead of owning-up to this feeling of sadness, the person hits out at others to alleviate it, ending up feeling further isolated and miserable — and minus the support of friends.

You need to become aware of what is going on inside you and identify what the feeling is. If it's a bad feeling, discover the cause. If there is an obvious cause, such as bereavement or illness, this can be dealt with. Similarly, if you have done something that makes you feel guilty or ashamed, you need to rectify this either by resolving the situation — or perhaps by accepting that you have failed to meet the standards you set for yourself. We all need to learn to relate to our good feelings and recognise that it is better to feel comfortable and relaxed than ecstatic.

Sometimes you cannot handle the strength of your feelings. You can fear that they are going to topple you and send you spinning out of control. This often leads you to avoid situations that leave you feeling vulnerable, threatened or frightened. Uncontrollable anger, for instance, can turn a mild disagreement into an emotional storm.

PAIN

Some feelings can be very painful, but remember that with time and effort the pain can be banished. Attraction to painful feelings can be the result of not having experienced good feelings for long enough. Some people begin to believe that pain is preferable and can only consider good feelings as something very temporary, that can be whipped away at any time. For such people pain remains because they have built up a closer association with it.

You have to realise that life is a combination of good and bad, both pain and pleasure. Once you recognise this you can work towards achieving a good balance. Learn to recognise when you feel comfortable and uncomfortable within yourself. Learn to make friends with your feelings and not to supress emotions. Your feelings are your most personal possession, and you must get to know them at every level. It is important to integrate your feelings into other aspects of your life.

CONFLICT

Sometimes unexpected situations arise causing people to feel conflict. For example, Mary has just received word that her sister has had a baby. She's thrilled and is especially happy that she has been asked to be godmother to the new arrival. Soon afterwards, Mary bumps into James, who has just learned that his father is very ill. Mary feels she cannot share her happy news with him and immediately shifts gear in order to empathise with him.

Anyone in control of their feelings can shift gear very quickly to suit the occasion. A person who is not in touch with his/her feelings finds it more difficult to change gear and may become resentful that the situation isn't suiting them.

Feelings are linked with your thoughts for that moment. You have to recognise what is going on and appreciate how other people feel. If you are content within yourself, the appropriate response will come spontaneously. You will automatically respond in a way that is comfortable for both yourself and the other person. You will only feel uncomfortable when threatened or when you feel in danger. Fear can make you freeze and unable to respond.

Certain situations create feelings that none of us particularly like. Worry, for example, can leave us anxious and unhappy and we begin to respond in a negative, rather than a positive fashion. Guilt can also cause us to respond negatively.

DIGGING UP OLD FEELINGS

Why is it that some of us dig up old feelings? Maybe it is because they are the feelings with which we are most familiar. A fresh bout of guilt, for example, can resurrect a past experience with a similar feeling. Instantly playing back old feelings is not allowing yourself to enjoy and be in tune with present experiences. Sometimes, there can be a pay-off for remaining stuck with a familiar feeling. If the feeling is negative you know you are going to experience a familiar pain that automatically has you seeking attention. The feelings associated with self-pity are a good example of this. On the other hand, revisiting good feelings can give rise to sensations of contentment. However, you must be careful not to confuse fantasy with reality.

Fantasy allows each of us to conjure up images to suit unfulfilled needs. On the other hand, reality confirms the real feeling of satisfaction or hurt. The reason some people remain in fantasy land is because the hurt feeling can be too painful. Turning our back on reality in favour of fantasy has its dangers. Basically, we're trying to convince ourselves that everything is OK. Sometimes living in fantasy can compensate for chaos in our lives. Reality, however, demands that we must do something about this chaos. Moving from chaos to stability means making changes — changes necessary in order to function and to feel comfortable within our own environment.

REJECTION

Everyone has experienced rejection to some degree or other. It really hurts and can leave a bitter aftertaste of humiliation. However, like a physical pain, there is always a remedy appropriate to the severity of the rejection. The answer is to act rather than re-act. Re-acting to situations on impulse, without thinking about what is going on, can leave you uneasy. You should cope with the bad and good in any situation. Remember that an extreme reaction of any sort is not healthy.

Some situations are particularly difficult. Often where rejection occurs you must get a fuller picture of what the real problem is. While the initial instinct is to look for a fault within yourself, a broader perspective may reveal a different perspective. For example, John feels rejected because he did not get a job that he dearly wanted. The rejection was a bitter blow to his ego as he felt he had the ideal personality and qualifications for the position. However, some time later, when he had gained more experience, he was able to look back and see how unprepared he would have been for the job.

FEELING GOOD

Sometimes we associate feeling good with the good times. In other words, we allow ourselves to feel good when everything is going well. However, everyone can learn to experience these feelings even when facing uphill battles. The secret is constantly affirming the positive, no matter how small. For example, even though your car won't start and you know you're going to be late for work, you can learn to cope in a way that maintains your positive feelings — by phoning to explain your dilemma rather than panicking and feeling that nothing will go right. Constantly coping in this manner means no matter how bad the situation, you know you can cope and therefore feel at ease and in control.

CHAPTER THREE

Relationships

Social relationships, casual relationships, friendships, kinships, best friends, intimate relationships, lovers, family, colleagues and marriages — all have to be worked at. They are demanding, time consuming, enjoyable and stimulating — and can at times cause pain and conflict.

However, we need relationships and many of us want to find out how to improve that special partnership.

You have a house, transport and perhaps a fairly rewarding job, but you each put thought, effort and money into acquiring life's necessities. You made decisions that involved choice and responsibility. You probably looked over several houses before deciding on a particular one. You test drove several cars, before buying a particular model.

It is hard work getting it all together, but you are generally happy to have put the time and effort into finding something that suits your particular needs. Likewise, relationships require a similar level of hard work and effort and finding a partner has its own price tag. In your search you can encounter confusion, pain and pleasure. You may have an image of the ideal partner. Many of us find our image has no foundation. It may be based on fantasy and illusion, akin to having a teenage crush on a beautiful movie star. Other people's ideas of a 'perfect' partner are based on past experience. People who have suffered from problematic parenting can often seek to fulfil childhood needs through a partner.

Then there are some people who fall in love with

someone they know to be not suitable for them, but cling to the hope that they can change their partner and bring them round to their own way of loving and thinking. The reality is that you can change yourself and your attitude to others, but you cannot change others.

It is often assumed that relationships will fall into place without work or effort. In truth, relationships demand hard work, commitment, good attitudes and compromise.

ONE TO ONE

We have all experienced the initial infatuation and attraction of a new love-affair. Missed heartbeats, clenched stomach muscles and starry eyes are all features of a new 'one to one' relationship. As the relationship progresses you have to adjust to your partner and your own needs, wants and beliefs. You must learn about the other person and yourself on several different levels. Total honesty, trust, commitment and a willingness to integrate changes experienced by both partners is necessary. No person stands still in a relationship. It's an ever changing process — moving forward, sometimes backwards. It's constantly in motion and both partners have to adjust to the pace.

THE REASONS RELATIONSHIPS FAIL

Very often one person's motivations in a relationship are entirely different to those of the other person involved. Failure can occur when the needs of neither partner are being met. One person may want excitement — the buzz of a new sexual encounter. The other may be craving love and stability. This is a definite mis-match. Then a lot of people confuse 'love' with 'being in love'. Some people are in love with the idea of 'being in love', never considering the reality and responsibility of a real relationship. A relationship can end very quickly when the reality of the situation becomes clear.

Playing games can be a survival technique for you if you are not ready to reveal your true self. However, some people feel safer playing games all the time in relationships even if another person's feelings are involved. It is an escape route used when intimacy of any sort appears in the relationship. In a trusting relationship where both partners are communicating easily with each other, they will take the rough times with the smooth, the bad with the good, striving, either consciously or unconsciously, to appreciate their partner despite any failings.

CONFLICT IN A RELATIONSHIP

In any relationship there are periods of conflict and tension. Often people avoid conflict by refusing to sit down and talk about it. They fear that direct confrontation about difficulties will result in the termination of the relationship. Once aware of conflict in your relationship certain choices are available, depending on whether the conflict merits being brought out into the open. Maybe the issue doesn't relate to the current relationship, but to a past one. It could also be a problem relating to you, not your partner. You need to ask yourself some questions as you decide how to act.

The following are some guidelines:

1. Stay calm and ask yourself what are the possible consequences of bringing the issue out into the open. Pay attention to the timing of confrontation. Be sensitive to the other person's reactions and be prepared to listen to their point of view.

2. Make sure you both have uninterrupted air-time. Avoid talk that merely blames one another. Try to express your

feelings assertively, not aggressively. Be specific about the issue, listen to what is said — but also to what is not being said.

3. Realise that you can mis-interpret situations and be prepared to alter your opinions accordingly.

4. Look for any hidden agendas. Avoid unfair argument tactics. Don't play games with such behaviour as guilt, sulking and the sending of threatening messages.

5. Simply state your feelings on the particular issue and then try to evaluate what is going on. Look for a solution, rather than create another problem.

LOOKING AFTER OURSELVES

In a relationship you also have to look after your own physical and mental welfare. If you don't look after yourself then how can you possibly expect others to do it? You should learn to treasure yourself; it is most important to keep up with your individual interests, so that neither partner in the relationship feels smothered. Having other interests and friends can strengthen a relationship, because both partners are bringing more to it.

A relationship should be stimulated and nourished, constantly. However, having too high expectations, sets you up for disappointment. Constantly planning and pushing risks shove your partner in the opposite direction. Allow the relationship to develop naturally.

SEEKING HELP WHEN THINGS GO WRONG.

Can a relationship be saved when things go wrong? The answer is yes, provided the damage is not irreparable. Often you don't work at saving a relationship because

Tantrums

Sulks

doing so demands that you face your own mistakes and misbehaviour. Professional help, such as seeking out a counsellor, can help — provided you listen to what they have to say. A counsellor cannot save your relationship. Only you can do that. Sometimes you must face up to the fact that a relationship is over. Remember it is always possible to enter another relationship when you are ready.

IMMATURE BEHAVIOUR

Immature people usually get involved in immature relationships. Their behaviour may be very extreme — tantrums and the like. You cannot behave in this fashion and expect your partner to respond in a mature way. It just doesn't make sense.

Shyness

Overwhelming

16

Every individual must look at his or her own behaviour and, if necessary, be prepared to adjust and grow, because a relationship is a combination of both peoples' strengths and weaknesses. Some people do decide to stay 'solo'. Perhaps they are frightened of revealing themselves so intimately to another person or perhaps they prefer a free, unattached state.

BARRIERS

Entering into an intimate relationship can be frightening. You've met, had a few dates and you're wondering where it goes from here. It can stay static in that you decide to just enjoy each others' company and only reveal a certain amount of information about yourself. To take a relationship further you must start disclosing more about yourself and this can leave you feeling vunerable and less independent — particularly if you have been previously hurt. Defence mechanisms of various sorts are likely to come into play at this stage. You may erect barriers in a bid to prevent your partner from getting to know you better. You and your partner must work to break down these barriers if the relationship is to continue. You both must allow time to gently remove your obstacles, if you consider the relationship to be worthwhile. Partners can do this by disclosing more about themselves and hope that you will follow suit. They can do this by giving you time and space and by letting you know that they trust you.

THE TOOLS OF A GOOD RELATIONSHIP

Qualities like honesty, loyalty, dependability, trust, communication and humour are just some of the necessary ingredients for a lasting and satisfying relationship. These are particularly important when the relationship enters a more intimate phase.

THE STRENGTH OF OUR FEELINGS

Many people long for closeness, but their fear of intimacy forces them to choose a distant stance in the relationship. Life involving closeness means looking at ones own sexuality. Some people get emotionally involved very quickly, not realising what is really demanded of them. This can be dangerous, akin to getting into the deep end of the pool when you can't swim. Basically, they are out of their depth and the struggle to surface can be a painful one, with an everlasting wound that cries 'never again'.

Like learning to swim, intimacy and emotional involvement have to be taken gently and responsibly. Intimacy is the seal on a relationship with another human being. There is a whole mystery surrounding a relationship at this level, because each person is having a very strong effect on the other. In a way each person is striving to find his or her identity. If an individual is trying to find their identity at the expense of another, very often the relationship will not last.

Over-involvement can smother the other person to the extent of suffocation and usually one person bails-out of the relationship. The healthy route to emotional involvement requires maturity on the part of both individuals and an appreciation of their own self-worth, combined with honesty and openness.

POSTPONING STRONG FEELINGS

Sometimes feelings can be so strong or you may feel so constrained by a situation that you postpone your feelings. You may consider it inappropriate to show anger at work, so you bring it home with you and take it out on your nearest and dearest. You may erect barriers in order to hide your feelings. Perhaps you are afraid of others seeing the real you. There are different levels of feelings, which are appropriate to different situations. The feelings involved in a platonic friendship are often very different to those of a passionate love affair. Confusion can result when you get the different levels mixed up and the feelings experienced are not appropriate to the situation.

The chemistry that attracts you to someone is necessary for a good relationship — but it is not enough to ensure that a relationship works. A good relationship is like a great friendship and demands the same kind of commitment. The two people respect each other and they don't place excessive demands on each other. There are no hard and fast conditions.

However, a relationship based on lust is a totally different situation; often the sexual, intimate stage is reached without ever having developed a relationship. You haven't gone through any of the normal stages of a relationship. The passion can burn itself out, the bubble can burst and you discover that you have little or nothing in common with the other person. Lustful behaviour can also indicate that a person is not interested in getting involved in a relationship. Perhaps they're only out for the sexual thrill. This can be confusing and destructive for the other person involved. They may be searching for love and may have confused passion for commitment.

HEALING A BROKEN HEART

The key to healing a broken heart is realising that recovery is possible. A broken heart at fifteen can often be mended more quickly than at fifty. But no matter what the age, some positive steps can be taken to get your heart back in loving order.

1. Acknowledge the loss. Don't bottle up your feelings.

2. Allow yourself time to heal.

3. Make contact with friends and keep up interests.

4. Avoid going into a new relationship on the rebound.

5. Accept that it's OK to be alone.

6. Look after your health.

7. Take up a new hobby or pastime.

8. Let go of the past and face the future with courage based on a new motivating force.

9. Seek professional help if your situation does not improve.

Broken-heart Department

Shyness is a form of stage fright, where you wonder if you can perform or if you're performing adequately. Being shy is a 'social anxiety' that is sometimes linked to approval-seeking behaviour. Basically, it hinders your ability to communicate in social settings where meeting new people can be very stressful.

Here are some methods to overcome shyness.

1. Learn to relax — e.g. via yoga, tapes, breathing exercises.

2. Make a list of all unrealistic rules which contribute to you being uncomfortable and shy — e.g. "I feel inadequate. Everyone else copes much better".

3. Assess these rules.

4. Change your rules if necessary to suit you.

5. Be flexible, allow yourself to make a mistake.

6. Learn to like yourself and express preferences rather than demands.

7. Go on a personal development or assertiveness course.

Still shy

CHAPTER FOUR

Communication

Effective communication demands energy as you try to make yourself understood. In order to have this energy it is up to each of us to nurture and nourish ourselves on every level—mentally, emotionally and physically. When you are drained, the signals you send out are weak and those receiving them will respond in a similar manner. In effect, your communication system has broken down. However, sometimes you don't know which part of your system is causing the problem. You could be having problems articulating, listening or absorbing.

Communication, like all effective systems, should be serviced on a regular basis, but you must be clear about what part needs servicing. For example, you may have no difficulty communicating with your boss or colleagues, but have great difficulty communicating on a one to one basis with loved ones at home. You may be a fantastic carrier of messages for others, but cannot convey any of your own.

FORMS OF COMMUNICATION

Speech is the most obvious form of communication, but is certainly not the only form of conveying messages. Touch is your first ever form of communication. As children we instinctively reached out and made contact. Certain emotions and feelings are also powerful communicators. Tears, laughter, anger and frustration can be communicated to others, using both visible and audible means.

Even when you are ill your ability to communicate does not wane. Your whole demeanour commutes the message that you are sick. Body language can be varied in order to communicate a message. Movements can reveal discomfort, shyness, confidence — even arrogance. And what you don't say, rather than what you do, can also convey messages, especially if the tone and inflection of your voice is changed to suit the particular occasion.

Communicating by silence can be a very powerful medium. A person who keeps their distance is communicating their message as effectively as someone who is over affectionate. Remember extremes of any nature are unhealthy, but you should not be afraid to experiment with your communications system. You can put your communication to the test by creating situations — situations, that others may find uncomfortable. You can, for example, convey a message that you know to be the wrong one, hoping to convince the other person that it's the right one. In effect you're fufilling your own need at the expense of others.

LISTENING AND REFLECTING

We tend to regard communication as the sending out of messages. But, a good communicator is someone who has the ability to also listen and reflect, to interpret messages and put them into perspective. A good communicator not only has the ability to deliver messages, but also has the ability to make sense of another's messages, no matter how vague they may be. They can communicate with the worst of communicators, whether in a professional or more intimate situation.

It is important to remember that children are forming a communication system at every level. They are learning about touch, language, texture, sound, and smell. They're learning how to communicate their needs to those around them and it is important that adults don't expect a child's communication network to run smoothly from day one. Everthing is trial and error. Allow children test out their systems. Give them freedom and allow them make mistakes. However, help them repair with a little gentle guidance. This helps them build the foundation for an effective communications system, which is the future keystone for relationships of every kind.

IN TOUCH

When you think of communication you think of getting in touch with someone, perhaps by telephone or letter. You send out a message and hope it is received and returned. Effective communication depends on everything being in good working order, whether it is a matter of the phone, postal system or whatever. But, the sender's communication system must also be in good working order. Indeed, we all send out clear messages when we feel good about ourselves. When feeling positive we also tend to listen to like-minded people and we recognise and cast aside negativity.

Effective communication demands that you are in touch with yourself; after all, your messages won't be clearly understood if your transmission is in any way fuzzy. The first thing is to get in touch with your thoughts and feelings. Determining your own self-worth is a demanding process, because often there is something that you don't want to face up to — something that makes you feel guilty, anxious or threatened. You mustn't be afraid to dig a little deeper — avoiding the temptation to give the standard answering machine reply. Your emotions must not hinder your ability to get in touch with yourself. After all, there is no point in trying to put a call through to someone else if your own line is full of static.

Communicating involves taking a risk with other people. You risk them knowing certain things about yourself and you risk being rejected. However, people that are in contact with their 'system' will have suffered previous rejection, dealt with it and be willing to take risks. Rejection is obviously not what anyone wants, but it is possible to cope. Even those lucky people who have never experienced rejection will cope. The secret is to like yourself and value your own self worth.

HAVING A GOOD BACK-UP SERVICE

It is important that people have a good back-up or support service in the event of a break-down in their communication network. It is vital that something else will support you at times when you feel vulnerable, weak — perhaps even intoxicated. Knowing your limits and thresholds is the key in the creation of a personal back-up service. You must learn to realise when you have exhausted a situation. Know when to leave well enough alone. And know when to say NO.

MIXED MESSAGES

Those, of either sex, who indulge in flirting, are prone to sending out mixed messages. People who flirt are experimenting with their sexuality in a light-hearted manner, but sometimes flirting is a veil that descends to cover fears and believed inadequacies. Flirting can, in fact, be employed as a barrier to cover up a feeling of 'I'm out of my depth'. It is a protective layer that enables you to be friendly with everyone and intimate with no-one. Flirting also confuses those on the receiving end. They're receiving a mixed message. It's very hard for someone on the receiving end to interpret the real message.

Sometimes you need to tread cautiously and adjust to this experimentation stage gently. Once you feel comfortable you can then progress rather than staying in an unclear flirtatious situation.

HOW TO GET YOUR COMMUNICATION SYSTEM IN ORDER

It is important that you like yourself and feel comfortable with your own communication system, so that the messages you send out are positive ones. By learning to listen to yourself you can become more aware of the messsages you sent out and can avoid sending out mixed messages. You can create the operational rules through deciding what thoughts and emotions you want to reveal.

You learn to control your output of both thoughts and emotions with knowledge and experience and in doing so you become ultimately responsible for your actions and behaviour.

Your own communication system can be efficient and smooth-running, and you can make sure that you don't isolate yourself for fear of getting close to others. After all, communication is a two-way process. The enjoyment comes from sharing with someone else and even sorting out the odd crossed wire.

RULES

The governing rule is that you take responsibility for your own comunication network. You cannot go through life apologising for mis-communicating. You can opt out and use all sorts of excuses, such as 'I was drunk' or feeling 'not quite myself'. What you really should do is to recognise the faults in your network and set about repairing them.

CHAPTER FIVE

Negativity v Positivity

Some people sail through life in a happy go lucky fashion. The sun rises, shines and goes down peacefully. Opportunities are there to be exploited and options are always available for consideration. These are positive people, who like themselves and behave accordingly. Such people live with solutions not problems, believing that effort is rewarded. The confidence that such people possess is an inner strength that has been achieved despite possible put-down, rejection and threats to their security.

The events that bombard all of us daily are seen by people with a positive outlook as a challenge, rather than a possible set-back. No task is too big to be tackled. They give it their best-shot. Everything is seized at the right moment and mistakes are looked on as a valuable learning process. Issues are dealt with as they happen. Positive people do not allow emotional baggage to obstruct their pathway through life.

Positive people attract other positive people. They radiate a visible contentment. They have an awareness of where they are; what they can do and what to expect; where they want to be and how to get there. They also recognise their own limitations, their strenghts and weaknesses. They know how not to make excuses and how not to blame others. Basically, they are in control of their own lives, which leaves them in good stead to shape their destinies. Negative people on the other hand are easily sucked into the never ending merry-go-round of negative thinking. They are usually the victims of their own circumstance and efforts. In fact, some may even like playing the victim role. They suffer from low self-esteem and can indulge in the poor-me syndrome. They complain that nothing ever goes right. They feel that the world and its people exploit them. They believe that their efforts are never rewarded — they don't even get to collect the consolation prize. The world is wrong; the system is wrong; friends and family are wrong.

They are suspicious, because they dislike themselves and others. They never move forward. There are no opportunities to be exploited. No solutions when things go wrong.

Negativity breeds negativity. Very often there are no answers, because the negative person doesn't search for them. They prefer to live in their problematic world and often they seek out other negative people as a form of survival. Together they refuse to let go of the past and relive former failures. They're constantly on play-back — their mental tape-recorders re-run nightmares of yester-year. Manipulation becomes a side-kick, as they create situations likely to cause further chaos and conflict. Family and friends can become foes, because they offer constructive advice. The destruction of oneself is often a likely possibility for negative people. Basically, they are confused and static.

WHY BE NEGATIVE

Many people become negative when their self-esteem is rock bottom and they don't recognise their own self worth. Feelings of negativity may come about through hidden thoughts or there may be deep-seated reasons — perhaps past experiences. Somewhere along the line you may have lost the ability to sort out the logic of messages. For instance, children who are constantly told that they are stupid may become stuck with that message, never believing that they can grow emotionally.

HOW DO I GO FROM BEING NEGATIVE TO POSITIVE

Finding the key to unlock the doors to opportunity, advancement, relationship stability, respect and friendships means moving from negative to positive and this demands adjustment and effort. Some of us will decide it's easier to stay locked behind those negative doors and will freeze when it comes to putting the key into the lock. Sadly, there is no escape for some people. Fear of change and the unknown keeps them immobile. Fear of what is on the other side of the door outweighs their discontentment. They prefer the familiarity of their (negative) life. These people risk ending up in life's assortment of discontented people.

Negativity can also come about by holding fast to familiarity. You may feel afraid of change so it becomes easier to decide to stay put, rather than reach out and sample unknown territory. It is like a child holding on to a much loved teddybear. It may be grubby and tattered, but it is familiar and makes them feel secure and safe. A new bear may appear attractive, but the problem arises when the old has to be discarded in favour of the new.

MOBILISING YOURSELF

When moving from negative to positive you must take things very slowly. Be gentle with yourself. Recognise areas of negativity and decide to give them the boot — one by one. Now you are ready to stop the old behaviour and bring in the new. You need to realise that you are moving into the unknown. You must be patient and call in the support of others. You must take the risk of making mistakes while being mindful of rejection. You must not let it topple you. Negative thinking must not creep into your thought processes. Listen for it and catch it before it sets down roots.

Although you may look for hidden meanings, often they don't exist. You must not be threatened by challenge. Instead you should be exploiting opportunities, but remaining mindful of other's feelings.

Often negativity comes about through weighty emotions. Guilt and worry are two of the biggest offenders. They threaten to anchor you, to keep you shackled. Become aware that you can lift your anchor at any time. You can be flexible and mobile. Like a ship you can call to other ports and set down a new anchor. Your journey to the positive port may demand that you navigate many obstacles.

You have to decide to overcome them, rather than letting them get the better of you. The idea is to keep your eye firmly fixed on your new destination — don't look back. Focusing on what you can do, rather than what you can't is a positive approach. Stay away from negative forces, such as people who want to make waves or situations that make you feel 'sea' sick. Decide that you are in control, but that you can call on your ship mates at any time for help and support.

Life is like a series of different ports and each person chooses at what ones to set down anchor. Strange ports will appear a little bit scary at times, but remember that everything becomes familiar. Realise the full potential of every port of call. Lift your anchor when negativity sets in and move to a new port where there will be new and positive horizons. Remember your 4 P's:

1. Be patient;
2. Get things in perspective;
3. Make preparations;
4. Pace yourself.

CHAPTER SIX

Rhythm and Blues

Monday morning dawns with a grey sky and promise of rain. You look out the window and decide that the weather is a suitable reflection of your own mood. You snuggle back on the pillows, throw the duvet over your head and make the decision to stay put. Everything is grey and you feel blue. Maybe the cause is the fact that it's Monday. You don't want to draw the curtain on a relaxed and enjoyable weekend and getting on with the task of work. Perhaps the bad weather is an excuse to stay in bed. Maybe a few more hours of blissful sleep is all that is needed or perhaps carrying out a certain task or meeting a difficult deadline is causing that nervous feeling.

Many of us have experienced this feeling of 'being down'. It is a combination of familar negative thoughts that threaten to take hold. The grey cloud of Monday morning is hovering overhead, ready to descend at any moment. But, you have choices. You can ignore it or allow it to descend. Those who do not allow it to take hold will get on with living and carry out their day's work. It was Monday morning; the weekend was over; it was a dull day . . . but now the tasks at hand can be tackled. In the end, such people decide not to let outside influences determine their mood for the day. They choose to behave in a confident manner and to deal with life's daily trials— traffic jams, irate colleagues, nagging spouses, crying children, bill demands and all the rest. They'll make the most of their day, perhaps realising that it could be their last. They will not let yesterday's downfalls and to-morrow's pitfalls interfere with their day.

Unfortunately, there are some people who have reason to feel sad or down. Grieving for a lost loved one; the break-up of a loving relationship; the end of a valued friendship and numerous other 'bereavements' cause them to re-act in a very subdued manner. This is a normal way to re-act — as long as it is not prolonged. If the feelings of sadness and gloom haven't lifted after a lenghty spell then professional help may be needed. The 'reactive situation' (where you are grieving an actual loss or the passing of something valued) is at risk of taking hold and leaving you bereft of happiness. You must take steps to keep hold of this happiness and seek other's help, advice and support when doing so. Seeking help, either from friends or professionals in the field, at an early stage is very important, as you can prevent the feeling of sad-ness from getting out of hand. You have to work towards your own happiness. You need never be afraid to admit you need help. In doing so you will have the support and admiration of others. Your own efforts combined with theirs will help put a smile back on your face.

Despondency can send your whole world crashing out of control. You feel down, guilty, ashamed and extremely unhappy. What was once seen as an opportunity is now considered an enemy. What was once a friend is now a foe. Places, people and things that once made you happy, now have no effect. Apathy is your companion and anxiety its cohort. Energy levels are low. Effort is considered pointless, as there's no light at the end of the tunnel. Indeed, effort seems almost impossible, as energy levels necessary to fuel physical, mental and emotional actions are just not available. What was once obtainable is now an endurance test.

Some people, however, have the ability to mask their doom and gloom. While they feel empty inside, their external image is more than presentable, because they are camouflaging their sadness and this is their way of coping.

RECOGNISING THE SIGNS

If despondency takes hold, it can cause sleep patterns to go haywire. Energy levels plummet. Concentrating on anything seems impossible. Interest in lovemaking, family, friends or work declines, the appetite suffers and nothing is going right. The enjoyment has literally gone out of living. Some people may feel an anger they cannot express. Instead of verbally hitting out, they turn the anger in on themselves and further increase the misery's hold.

One of the worst aspects of despondency is the feeling that things will never get better. You can't find the switch-off button. It seems like a bottomless black pit of despair. Expert help and the support of friends can help bring you back from the brink. There is no light at the end of the tunnel, until you set about finding it. The first step in your recovery is recognising that you have a problem — that you are despondent. The second step of recovery is having the courage to seek help.

Sadness can take the guise of physical ailments — indeed physical illness can stem from despondent orders, as your physical, mental and emotional welfare all suffer. Headaches, aches and pains, indigestion, ulcers and a host of other ailments can result from despondency and some people find it easier to seek medical treatment for these disorders rather than seeking help for their underlying cause — misery. It is easier to say 'I have a pain in my stomach' than 'I'm feeling very low' — it seems more socially acceptable.

Unhappiness is less tangible than a physical ache — therefore, it is harder to deal with. When feeling low you may feel totally helpless. You cannot point to the pain. Two pain killers won't numb the aching void. It is, therefore, critical to become aware of what is happening. You must be in constant touch with your mental and emotional states. Listen to what your body, thoughts and feelings are telling you. If you are feeling unhappy, there has to be a reason. It is up to each of us to try and rectify the situation and help the sun to shine again.

Perhaps you are overworked. You may just need to relax. Perhaps you are stressed and need to take time out to look at your situation. Perhaps you are undervaluing your personal or professional worth and need to realise how important you are. Perhaps you are underselling your talents and are therefore feeling hard done by — only you can change this particular situation. Perhaps you feel sad because you've just broken-up with someone special. Perhaps you have lost someone dear to you and have not yet come to terms with their departure. Perhaps you are devoting your time to everyone else's problems and not allocating any time to sit back and deal with your own.

Whatever the problem, each of us needs time and space to deal with it. Any sense of loss brings about sadness and feelings of despair. However, healing will come, aided by the support of others and the knowledge that things will get better.

WHAT IF I'M NOT HEALING

Sometimes you may feel down, yet there is no sign of healing — then the sadness has gone very deep. Therapeutic help is needed, either on a one to one basis or in a group situation. Like a physical illness, mental and emotional upheavals are treatable. Recovery takes place with the correct treatments and a period of recuperation. Strive to be patient. Be kind to yourself. Be aware that everyone has a duty to look after their mental and emotional wellbeing and needs. You need not be afraid to admit to having a problem. Talk to someone. Admitting your fears and asking for help is an important step. The chances are that they've been through something similar and will be a companion on the road to recovery. Trying to maintain a sense of balance is important. Don't let resentments and undue anxieties get out of hand —and don't let them get hold of you.

AVOID WEARING LABELS

Labelling yourself can be unhelpful. Avoid sayings like 'I'm a born worrier'; 'I always expect the worst'; 'I can't change the way I feel'; 'nothing goes my way'. Try and say 'I'll try', rather than 'I can't'. Keep doing this and soon you will believe in yourself and won't leave

yourself open to exploitation, nor will you continue to find
yourself in a slotted position.

PREVENTION IS BETTER THAN CURE

Feeling good about yourself means that you are better
equipped to cope in any situation. Developing good coping skills helps to keep the blues at bay, and this can be
reinforced by improving communication skills. As an
individual, look at where you are and where you want to
be. Examine your position in the family and look at your
relationships, whether they be with family, friends, colleagues or lovers. Examine whether your needs are being
met and seek to fill those that remain unfulfilled.

Remember there is always something you can do to
make a situation more comfortable for yourself. Even
small steps may be painful in the beginning but realize
that it is probably necessary to suffer in order to gain.
Discovering what your strenghts and weaknesses are and
nurturing the positive enables you to discard the negative.
You should stick to your limitations — aiming too high
only causes stress. Unobtainable expectations will only
cause you grief. If you are always ready to face life's
challenges and never afraid to ask for help, you will be
better able to enjoy your discoveries and recognise, but
quickly forget, your failures.

POINTERS

Turn your back on the 'rewind syndrome' — where you
allow your mind to repeatedly play over old mistakes and
failings. They are in the past, so why keep digging them
up. Yesterday is over, today is a fresh beginning and
tomorrow is another chance.

Remember it is not conceited to love yourself. It is essential in order to be loved by others. Maintaining your own well-being is of great benefit to others, because you will have time to spend with them and help them nurture theirs.

Study each situation and decide what contribution you have to make.

Don't be afraid to investigate new fields. Be open to new ideas and interests.

Take one step at a time. You must learn to walk before you can run.

Listen to others and expect them to listen to you.

Aim to discard useless guilt and worries. Guilt will only slow down your progress in new matters.

Don't be afraid to give your opinion, but be open to the response. And never be afraid to speak out if you feel criticism coming your way is unwarranted or unfair.

Don't let others do your thinking for you. Ask their advice, but don't expect them to come up with all the answers.

Enjoy life. Don't feel guilty about taking time out. Life is for living. Don't let it pass you by.

CHAPTER SEVEN

If the 'CAP' fits . . .

A t different stages of your life you wear different caps — caps fitting to suitable ages and roles. However, for some the cap never fits correctly and you end up compensating, instead of tailoring the size. Compensation comes variously packaged. The initial compensation might come in the form of a little treat — a drink, a cigarette. Usually one form or other of tasteful stimulation is the compensator — sugar, even chocolate can do the trick.

Some people can stop at the little treat, but for others it doesn't stop there and the little treats become an essential crutch. Eventually some people end up using their compensationary crutch to overcome every difficulty experienced. The compensation factor becomes the tool with which to eliminate the pain of any situation, whether it be from anxiety, tiredness or stress. Initially, the little treat scenario may work. An alcoholic drink often helps relax us, especially when we feel stressed or out of sorts. Alcohol, after all, is a pleasurable toxin. It has its place. It only becomes a problem when abused and exhalted to the position of controller. Often the one alcoholic drink leads to another. Soon the original problem, which resulted in you taking a drink has become a dual-edged sword with the drinking itself becoming problematic.

When an uncomfortable feeling arises, your first instinct is to get rid of it, but how do you go about doing this? Very often time is the only healer, but the impatient person cannot wait and chooses to numb the feeling via their chosen mode of compensation, whether it be drink, drugs or food.

Then other problems — sidekicks of the chosen compensation — will start building up. Alcohol dependency, for example, may result in an inability to cope with everyday problems. Eventually there will be out of character behaviour and breakdown of relationships. Personal appearance will also suffer and the person is likely to suffer from financial and perhaps legal problems. If you get into this state, it is likely the addiction has taken over and you are controlled by the compensation, that is, drink, rather than taking control of your own life.

Compensatory factors very often allow you to excuse yourself from real living. You'll make excuses that the factor is controlling you. For example, a choc-a-holic will become so fat that they'll probably decide to opt-out of things, because they'll feel less confident.

On the other hand, a drug addict has little real choice. Their addiction limits them from using any of their own resources with which to function. The chemical resource, whether it be crack or cocaine, distances them from reality and they just manage to exist. The drink or drug addict can also allow themselves to live in a world of fantasy and illusion. When reality finally sets in, so does the cruel realisation that they have hit rock bottom. The repair and healing process can now begin — that's if it's not too late.

TURNING POINT

For some there can be a turning point. The person who realises that they've become addicted must also realise that they have a personality which lends itself to compulsion. Compulsive people usually want everything done immediately. They are extremely impatient. They constantly project into the future and allow past mistakes to haunt them. Very often they never have a sense of their real selves, because it is hidden deep in the bottle or the next fix.

Their vision of themselves is blurred to the extent that they have lost sight of who or what they are. Only when they emerge from their addiction will they realise and accept their limitations, expectations and realisations. They will have paid a high price, but everything need not be lost — professional help and treatment can restore people's health. They can emerge and start living again.

However, they must treat their addiction as a poison — as a cruel enemy, not a thoughtful friend. There will always be moments when the temptation will be there to return to old habits, but they must realise that they have the ammunition to fight off this enemy — namely their belief in themselves and the help and support of others. They can call on long dormant resources or those which have never been tapped — resources that will enable you to deal with the situation, rather than reach for the compensationary crutch.

Often you need the promise that things are going to get better. Indeed often you cannot get only worse, so the only way is up. It's important to see light at the end of the tunnel — it gives you something to move towards. An awareness of your addiction and the patient passage of time will help you take control.

Realise that boredom can be stemmed. Yes, time drags and you want to alleviate the sense of nothingness. Using a chemical, like drink, gives a quick but, unfortunately, a false sense of control. Chemicals only energise your behaviour system for a short time, that is until the next fix. These fixes mask your real feelings and wants. They give a false sense of confidence. You believe nothing can take you down or get the better of you. Most of us have been there, while under the influence. You are better for having confidence, and this is the seemingly sensible rationale,

FINEST CRUTCHES

I don't know where I'd be without my crutches!

that can prompt you to over-indulge in alcohol.
problem is finding the delicate balance between what is
enough and what is too much. As an individual gains
confidence he/she often loses the ability to stop at a point
where confidence is attractive or down right awful. The
temptation to have another drink increases with intoxi-
cation and you risk ending up out of control.

With the addict this is a constant and vicious circle. The
compulsive person doesn't know where to call a halt. So
the wheels of recovery can only be set in motion when the
addict becomes aware that they have a problem; recognise
that they and others are suffering because of it and decide
to call a halt.

It's important to remember that crutches, like alcohol,
are really depressants, not stimulants. Only the initial
effect is one of stimulation. Over-indulgence affects you
physically, mentally and emotionally — and there is
always the worry of not knowing what situation you
became involved in while under the influence. Mean-
while, it has become socially unacceptable to blame your
behaviour on crutches, such as drink. The consequences
are too great, that is, drink driving and casual sex. You do
not want your personality to become subject to your
addiction.

Remember if you are over indulging in any one
particular item, stop and seek help immediately. You
could be a very good friend to yourself if you avoid that
destructive path early on.

he Games We Play

As a child you began to experiment with play. Most forms of play were instinctive, while other forms were learned. Often you played alone, using your imagination. Other times you played alongside friends using combined imaginations to create exciting fantasies. Then there were the structured games and then ones where you had to learn rules and regulations. You had to adhere to the rules if you were to partake and even win.

It is easier to role-play fantasies and be spontaneous when you are young. You become more inhibited as you grow older and tend to follow a structured theme. In other words, you learn the rules in order to achieve and win. In a work situation, for example, the aim is to succeed and sometimes your inclination is to be spontaneous, to use your initiative and be creative, even idealistic. However, sometimes it doesn't arouse your enthusiasm and your creativity isn't (you feel) getting the recognition and reward that it deserves. Your only remaining option, if you wish to stay put, is to learn the existing rules and follow them.

This can work for some people, provided there are no loopholes or hidden agendas. You wear the right/suitable style of dress; you talk to the right people; you say the right things and are seen in all the right places. Doing all this may go deeply against your personal beliefs and values, but you are aware that it is necessary behaviour in order to succeed. There are few outright winners and losers in the game of life — only adapters. Sticking to the rules in order to succeed demands a certain amount of effort and discipline, alongside a good thinking brain. You end up being honest with yourself rather than frustrated with game play. There are others who create their own rules as they go along. Often these people are able to convince others that these are the 'real rules'. In real life this policy manifests itself as manipulation.

Life, however, is not always about winning and losing — it is about living. Sometimes people get tired of using their energy playing games and decide to stop deceiving themselves. It may take some sort of a crisis to bring about this recognition; the person can now decide to take time out, sit back, and relax. Remember that in the end it really does not matter who succeeds. It is taking part that matters. Deciding that your life will be free of playing games and more full of play-time allows you to be spontaneous, enjoying surprises, space and you may even sparkle.

At school you were no use to the team until you understood the rules. Likewise having understood the rules in professional life you can concentrate on your performance rather than bend the rules to suit your game. You need not be dishonest, scheming, and risk hurting others. Remember there are always others who may be more scheming than you and are, in effect, capable of undermining your personal confidence and status. It is possible to be seen as 'the best' and to win that much-sought-after promotion without risking the loss of support, respect and love of colleagues, family members and partners.

The only way to succeed happily is by adhering to recognised codes of behaviour and professional conduct putting your best efforts into your work and maintaining a cheerful and positive outlook.

RULES IN YOUR PERSONAL LIFE

Some people see life as a game — period. They do not curtail game-playing to the workplace; they bring it home

with them and threaten to cause all sorts of pain. These people only consider themselves as winners or losers. They even apply this formula to meaningful personal relationships. Hence the game of life which they 'win' is always at someone's expense where the price paid is pain.

Anger or annoyance can occur in a relationship where both partners are using a different set of rules. One person may be playing a game called 'fill my needs', while the other is indulging in a game called 'I don't know how to fill my own'. This kind of game-playing can result in a very strong power struggle, and usually the person playing the game of 'fill my needs' wins, because their rules are more powerful, more selfish.

Playing games in a relationship is especially dangerous, because ultimately someone gets hurt. And if both partners are playing games the chances are that the relationship will not flourish, as each will update and rewrite their own set of rules to suit their own particular needs.

AFFECTION SEEKING GAMES

Affection seeking games are played both consciously and unconsciously and the rules are often written using childhood experiences as a foundation to begin from. Unfortunately the two people involved may be coming from different starting points and their lines never intersect. It is like putting together a jigsaw, only to discover that vital pieces are missing and the picture can never be complete.

At this stage the couple should abandon their individual agendas and find a mutual one from which to launch a new agenda — that is if they are both willing. This can be a demanding, emotional and painful process; however, the effort is rewarding. It can pay dividends in that you end up being with one another, rather than suffering from dishonesty and isolation.

For example, Mary and John have just started dating. Each would like to form a relationship, but the friendship cannot go further and is being constantly distracted by John's friends and work and Mary's need for expensive meals and gifts.

In other words while Mary and John may look the perfect couple neither is being totally honest and while their social life seems full, their private emotional needs are being starved.

HOW DO I STOP PLAYING GAMES

Becoming more aware of your own strengths and weaknesses is important. Look on both as potential resources. You can create your own tools with which to cultivate these resources. These tools can take the form of increased self confidence or esteem; a better communications system and an increased recognition of your own and other's needs.

If you believe in yourself others will soon follow suit. You can have a positive outlook that realises your potential; avoid those who only want to play games, rather than perform their duties.

CHAPTER NINE

Controlling your life

Let's look at how you learned to drive. First you had to get lessons, either from a friend or a professional. Then you needed a car in which to practise. Most people don't like lending their four wheeled pride and joy to a novice, so you probably had to save up and buy an old banger.

At this stage, you have learned the basics. You know how to operate the controls — the clutch, accelerator, brake and gears. Now you are ready to move from your driveway out onto the main road. This move demands putting trust in other people, namely motorists and pedestrians. You have learned the rules of the road and hope that others will stick to them and give you an even break.

You're nervous and are bound to make mistakes. Initially, the car may stall, gear change gets mixed up, the engine floods.

However, with a little patience and perseverance — combined with a little courtesy from others — you learn to control the car. Once out and about on the highways and byways, you experience a very strong sense of achievement, independence and control. Independent of public transport, you no longer have to beg lifts from others, getting from A to B without depending on anyone else. Yet there is always that one obstacle; a car can break down at any stage. However, the wise driver is already armed with the knowledge of how to change a wheel; and can tell the difference between points and plugs.

Taking control of your own life can be compared to learning to drive a car. You make a decision and take the necessary steps to achieve it. Sometimes you might have to master a new skill. You will also need support — someone to show you the technique until you are fully competent by yourself. Initially, you will make mistakes, but you should look on them as inherent to achieving your goals and taking control of your own destiny. Always anticipate what can go wrong, so that you can have a repair kit ready. You cannot totally depend on others. You can place trust in them, but you must be able to cope yourself. You can start by looking after yourself, eating decently, getting ample sleep and regular exercise.

Now look at other areas:

JOB: Is it where you want to be? Can you go further or can you switch lanes?

LEISURE TIME: Are you cruising at a leisurely pace or at breakneck speed. Decide to make better use of your leisure time or, if necessary, set some time aside for leisure and relaxation.

FINANCE: Examine how you handle money. Do you overspend? Are you living on credit? Or are you tight and afraid to spend, always waiting for that rainy day? Are you obsessed with money and consider it in preference to leisure, enjoyment or other people?

CONTROLLING YOUR FITNESS

There are many kinds of fitness, not just sport and exercise. It's important that you pay attention to other areas of fitness, including your nutritional supply, environmental conditions and your mental and emotional state. A lot of it is basic common sense.

Mental fitness demands taking control of your thinking process. First you must ask yourself some questions. "Am I a negative thinker, always expecting the worst? Do I get sucked into negative situations and am I attracted to negative thinkers? Am I so stressed that I cannot think?"

You should try to adopt a positive approach, projecting a positive image of yourself and setting short and long term goals. You can also aim to control the way you talk about yourself and others. Strive to adapt to change and still stay in control.

Taking control of your life helps ensure that you feel comfortable. You can be aware of obstacles and enjoy challenges. You can handle difficulties and refuse to allow setbacks to topple you.

It makes sense that a finely tuned engine will give a smoother spin than one rusty with neglect. A similar analogy applies to people. And in this case the complexities of a human being only add to the variety involved in the human fitness challenge.

THE INGREDIENTS FOR TAKING CONTROL

1. Look at where you are, what you have got, what you want and where you want to be.

2. Throw out the things that make you feel uncomfortable such as guilt and worry.

3. Decide what you want to change and start taking steps in that direction.

4. Realise that you are moving towards the unknown and that you may feel frightened and slightly panicked in the early stages.

5. Be aware that new situations are going to be created.

6. Examine any fears, worries or apprehensions you may have.

7. If you feel inadequate on your own, seek help with a friend or counsellor who will give you positive feedback.

8. Appraise your personal life and decide what influences you and how you influence others.

9. Stand back and look at what really is going on, rather than what you think might be going on.

10. Look at how you communicate with others — your language, body movements and eye-contact.

11. Don't be afraid to make mistakes and to suffer a little disappointment, setback and pain.

None of the above can be seriously attempted if you don't keep your energy levels topped up. Don't risk running out of steam. Relax and take a break when things start getting too much. Enjoy new discoveries and tackle problems sooner rather than later.

CHAPTER TEN

Building your own Self-Confidence

How you feel and how you think about yourself determines how you behave. When a person feels confident he/she will behave enthusiastically and assertively, will give out positive vibes and will take responsibility for their actions and choices in life. Their body behaviour reveals their message through open, firm and mobile physical movements. An assertive person recognises his/her own rights and takes responsibility for initiations and the resulting consequences. They also recognise their limitations and don't have unreasonable expectations of themselves.

Unfortunately, not everyone behaves in an assertive

manner. Some people are entirely passive, while others are aggressive. Passive people communicate in a very hesitant, quiet manner. They are usually lacking an awareness of their own self-worth. Sometimes passive people feel their rights are being violated and that they are always being pushed into the background. Their silence, which appears as sufferance, may be their way of manipulating others. Passive people allow others to depreciate them and they fast become push-overs. Aggressive people often get what they want, but always at the expense of others. They act in a superior manner and end up hurting other people by taking their rights away. They often feel they have a right to be aggressive and get rid of any inner anger. Sometimes those who behave aggressively are seeking revenge for a past slight.

In order to feel good about yourself, you must feel confident. You must make your own choices and still allow others to express their feelings and beliefs.

The cause of these different behaviour styles — passive and aggressive — can be traced as far back as childhood, but it is still no reason for you to behave in a manner that is inappropriate and uncomfortable for others.

A passive person will circle around an issue, never confronting it head on or dealing with it. An aggressive person attacks very early on in a hostile and often ruthless manner. The assertive person sees the issue for what it is and deals with it. They do not let bottled up feelings, such as anger and hurt, blur the picture.

WHAT IS ASSERTIVE BEHAVIOUR?

Being assertive involves recognising where you are at in life and being able to communicate at every level in a non-threatening or punishing way. It also means that you are able to ask, not demand, certain things, while remaining comfortable with yourself and others. You are also able to talk about yourself, accept compliments and disagree with unfair criticism. Assertive people are not afraid to take risks in life and do so without undue anxiety. Being assertive means being appropriate and comfortable with yourself. Knowing when to express a certain feeling, assertive people are aware of the appropriate social skills and don't apologise for giving their opinion.

Above all, assertive people recognise their own self-worth and they are aware of their rights as individuals. They can express an opinion and at the same time value another's. Assertive people do not avoid others through shyness, and they rarely come away thinking someone has taken advantage of them. Their confidence comes from an inner sense of well-being, both physically, emotionally and mentally. In relationships, assertive people are happy to initiate change, maintain that change and adapt to new circumstances.

HOW DO I BECOME ASSERTIVE

The step towards becoming assertive is to first examine your role in life. You should compare reality with your expectations. You must be willing to change. You need to examine how you behave and how you think about ourselves and others.

Someone whose thought process is negative needs to set about breaking this cycle. They must begin to take action, rather than reacting to others.

You must allow yourself to feel and you must not be afraid to label your feelings as it can help you recognise and understand them. Talking your feelings and fears over with a good friend, gives you important feedback. When we've done all this, you can start changing slowly.

Remember Rome wasn't built in a day. Be patient and deal with one issue at a time.

A useful place to start is by looking at what is expected of you in certain roles, whether professional or personal. You must respect yourself and take responsibility for whatever you think, say or do.

Eliminate negative language from your vocabulary. You also need to recognise your own needs independently of others and, above all, give yourself permission to make mistakes. You should enjoy your successes, no matter how small and never be afraid to ask others for clarification on matters you are uncomfortable or unsure about. Never be afraid to ask for extra time to think something over or don't be scared to question others.

You can set clear boundaries and decide what you want from a situation. Remember that you have a responsibility towards others and you should not violate their rights. Examine how you respond in various situations, whether among friends, colleagues, family or the public. Are you infuriated by other people's bad habits? Do you defend your actions when someone criticises you unfairly? Do you express your point of view? Do you always feel under a compliment to others?

RELAXATION

Once people decide to be more assertive, they need to relax and takes things slowly. Having decided what to do, you can repeat it over and over again until you feel comfortable with your decision. You must not get defensive or anxious if you find that others are re-acting in a hostile manner to your new image. You will have to learn to handle this hostility and be honest about your feelings, so that you begin to get comfortable with talking about yourself, ready to take the limelight. You should be open to discussing both your negative and positive elements, without fearing attack.

You can learn to attain workable compromises, avoiding judgemental attitudes and sarcasm. Patronising behaviour creates friction. You must look at your use of language, the tone and inflection of your voices. Do you mumble? What message does your body language and appearance convey? Does it inspire confidence in others?

You need to learn to say No and Yes in appropriate situations. You must learn to express your anger appropriately. Become aware of indirect power, that is, the power of others to charm or seduce you into a situation you find uncomfortable or distasteful. Refuse to listen to unfair criticism and harmful nagging sentiments. Also be open to change, be flexible, more relaxed and decide to enjoy even the small things. Finally, you should allow yourself to be spontaneous. It isn't necessary to weigh up the pros and cons of every situation. You can then feel free to enjoy yourself, others and your surroundings.

I'm always right

CHAPTER ELEVEN

Planning and Goal Setting

Setting goals is the first step towards planning your future. In order to create opportunities you must look at what you want to achieve in life. Goals help you to assess what is going on and how you can go about achieving what you want in life. Goals can be short term, medium or long term and setting them helps to create a balance in your life, especially if they are realistic and obtainable, yet challenging.

Goals can also be classified into personal — that is, those concerning family and partners, and professional objectives, those governing work and education. Before deciding on your particular goal or goals look at what time and energy you spend in relation to the following:

1. Your physical, emotional and mental health.

2. Your relationships.

3. Your career.

4. Value systems.

5. Your financial situation.

6. Education and the acquisition of knowledge.

As you grow older different interests in life will take precedence over others. For most people the three main interests in life will be their health, relationships and career.

1. HEALTH

This is the most important factor; without it none of the other categories are achievable. If you look after your physical health your mental and emotional health will usually correspond. Poor physical health will eventually lead to poor mental health and a neglected emotional system. No amount of money or material assets can substitute for a healthy body and mind. Looking after your health means eating well, getting ample sleep and adequate exercise. Keeping to this simple three point plan pays obvious dividends.

2. RELATIONSHIPS

How you feel about yourself and how you communicate with others dictates your emotional state. Personal growth in the area of relationships can be achieved successfully through goal-setting. You must also allow yourself space to evaluate these goals if you find that they are not proving successful, whether in the area of family or partners. Seek professional help if this area is causing you discontentment.

3. CAREER

It is often thought that a career chosen after school or college is a life-long one. However, it is possible to change occupations at any time. People can decide to have a multi-career. The important thing to remember is that you have options. If one job isn't suitable you can strive to move into something else. Those who are not presently employed also have options to consider: training courses, working at home versus working abroad, working with others versus starting a business or voluntary work to gain experience for that job down the road.

Some people determine their career according to their educational qualifications or training, while others determine it through experience. What you make of it is up to yourself, and money is not the only criteria for deciding on the sucess of a chosen career. There are other facets which are much more important.

Happiness and a sense of job satisfaction; a sense of purpose and a sense of achievement are often a lot more important than earning power. And if you are unhappy, either in terms of satisfaction or money, you can always change. You can open the doors of opportunity by learning new skills and testing your potential for growth. You should never be afraid to make a mistake. Instead, you should see mistakes as an opportunity to grow. Sadly, some people do stay in a particular job because of fear of change and failure. Often they end-up blaming the system for their unhappiness. You must be prepared to enter the unknown in order to bring about constructive change.

MAKING THAT CHANGE

Decide what you really want. Then start your programme for change with the help of the following guidelines:

1. Preparation: Examine whether your skills and abilities match those required for the new job. Maybe you need further qualifications or more experience.

2. Patience: Allow yourself time to acquire those specified credentials.

3. Presentation: Does your CV and interview image need improvement.

4. Positivity: Do you have a positive outlook.

5. Persistence: If you don't suceed on the first attempt, persist. Perhaps you need more time or your perception of the job was off-line.

4. VALUE SYSTEMS

You obtain your value systems from your culture, your race, your families and religion. They're usually handed down to us. But, as you grow/mature you often reject certain values and create ones of your own — hopefully within reason.

Your personal value system determines your priorities and subsequently your behaviour. You risk feeling frustrated, confused and guilty if you are in conflict with your personal value system. Indeed, goal-setting can become very difficult because what you are doing may be in direct conflict with your beliefs and value system.

It is important for you to combine harmoniously what is good for you with what is also good for others. It's about creating a balance.

5. FINANCES

Money, it is said, is the root of all evil. However, in this world if you want something you have to pay for it, usually with money. People acquire money in different ways. Most people earn it; others inherit it and many of us borrow it. There may be different methods of acquiring money, but everyone uses it to determine their lifestyle. If you gamble or drink it away, the chances are that you will have a bleak lifestyle. If it is wisely invested the outlook is more favourable.

It must be remembered that wealth does not guarantee happiness. Too much money can risk you getting wrapped up in a world full of material trappings and gadgets. You can neglect to nurture more important values, such as love, friendship and personal growth. Material things are a very poor substitute for real friendship and affection. Goal setting in the area of finances, whether it be deciding to spend less or more or to stop substituting spending power for communication with other people can pay real dividends. The ideal is to treat money wisely, with consideration of your health and happiness.

6. EDUCATION AND ACQUIRING KNOWLEDGE

Not alone have you a need for food, warmth and love, you also have a need for knowledge. Some of us however tend to overlook this particular hunger. For many, education stops the day they leave the classroom or finish that last exam. But education does continue outside school or college. Life is a learning experience, but it is not all about qualifications and exam results.

Experience is a wise teacher in the same way that books impart specialist knowledge. The beauty lies in being able to choose what you want to learn, in setting goals and following them through. You need to be mentally nourished through consumption of knowledge. Remember that you can bring your knowledge to any corner of the world. It is your constant companion.

CHAPTER TWELVE

Barriers, Blockages and Blunders

Few of us would turn down the offer of achieving perfection. Somewhere deep inside us is the wish to be the perfect human being. We want to be able to look well, feel well and relate well. We want the perfect partner, offspring, home, job and car. The odd thing is that we actually build barriers in a bid to achieve perfection. These barriers are erected to hide our real selves and to create a self we believe is acceptable to others. Some of us don't set out to build barriers, while others do so unconsciously. These barriers prevent us from reaching out to others and growing in any way.

Your defences are there to protect you from possible hurt. But you can also utilise your defences to hide the person. A person may find it difficult to express a deep emotion, so they disguise it with another, less threatening one. For example, a person who is seething with resentment may not want to put their inner anger on public display. Instead they adopt a 'don't care less' attitude, which is very effective at keeping others at arms length.

Sometimes you find yourself releasing pent-up office emotions at home — dangerous and damaging behaviour, both for yourself and others. Jealousy is another thing we are all pretty good at disguising. We don't want others to recognise our jealousy or envy, so we mask it in wit and sarcasm. Beware. Few people are fooled. You may have perhaps convinced yourself that your jealousy is well screened, because you don't want others to discover the resentment — it gives too much of an insight into what you believe are your own failings. You can only be jealous if you perceive that the other person has got something (or someone) you haven't.

Projecting blame is another barrier. You shift the blame of your mistakes onto the shoulders of others, hoping to take the pressure off yourself. You are also good at blaming mistakes on circumstances and inadequate equipment. Blaming others and things takes the limelight off us and prevents people from digging deeper.

Very often you dislike in others what you cannot accept in yourself. Sometimes you cannot recognise the thing you dislike in yourself, because you have suppressed it. You may not, for example, be particularly happy about your body shape, because you have a very poor self-image. Instead of working to change it, you spend your time criticising others to take the spotlight off yourself. It's another very effective method of disguising the inner self.

JUSTIFYING THE BARRIERS

The stronger the barrier, the harder you try to justify it. You actually create reasons for having erected it. Indeed you may have had an initial reason for erecting it, for example, a broken relationship. The barrier, which was meant to be temporary, has now become permanent, almost immobile.

EXAMPLES

You constantly press home the point that you enjoy your independence. The truth could be that you are afraid of intimacy and dependency. You avoid going for that promotion, claiming that you're happy where you are. The truth could be that you don't feel capable of doing the job or you're scared of making the necessary change. In all cases the truth is not faced.

I'M ALWAYS RIGHT

This is another barrier much utilised by those who, in fact, have deep doubts about themselves. Striving to convince others that they're always right is a powerful way of defending the ego against possible put-down and discovery of a damaged self.

THE PERFECT BODY AND MIND

A strange sounding barrier, but one none the less. You seek always to be perfect. You look immaculate and always seek to project the image of perfection. Often no-one gets in any way close to you. You fear that they will never match up in the perfection stakes. This can, in fact, be a very powerful barrier.

The intellectual barrier occurs where a person cannot move beyond the contents of his/her own head. Everything must have a reason. Everything must be logical. Everything must have an answer or a solution. They usually use their intellect, via language, to fend off people. It's a pretty effective method, as people often feel too inadequate or inferior to approach them.

There are people who have movable barriers, that is, the barrier is put in place when it is felt the situation requires it. This is a form of manipulation, as the barrier is erected in order to control a situation. Such people allow others to remove their barriers, but keep theirs up. Others can end up feeling hard done by or embarassed, fearing that they have told all, while the other person has kept silent.

Other people have more light-weight barriers — they flirt, for example. It appears that everything is quite care-free, even playful, but the barrier is there and helps maintain a distant relationship.

BLOCKAGES

Blockages arise from having too many barriers. They are different to barriers in that they are more rigid, more solid. Those people who've erected blocks are likely to use isolation as a protective measure. They have 'no-go' written all over them. They isolate themselves to the extent that people don't try to get to know them. It is often too difficult and people may feel that it is not worth the effort.

Blockages can result in people over-compensating. They are at pains to disguise their barriers, for fear people will discover why they were erected in the first place. The over-compensator is likely to become engrossed in solving everyone else's problems and tends to neglect or even ignore his/her own.

BLUNDERS

Most barriers and blocks eventually lead to blunders, because at some stage you don't cover your tracks and the real person emerges, warts and all. Few people want to admit to a blunder, because it means admitting that they have made a mistake. To own up to a mistake means that you are less than perfect! You may also need help to clear-up your blunder and this can be painful and humbling. It also means taking responsibility for and owning up to having blockages and barriers, which you feel are well disguised. The blunder lifts the lid. When the lid comes off, all is revealed and then you must start dealing with the consequences.

HOW TO DISMANTLE YOUR BARRIERS AND REMOVE YOUR BLOCKAGES

Often you have to be brave and ask someone else to reveal how he/she see you. Many of us are ignorant of our own blind-spots — it takes others to point them out, and this can be a very painful process. If you feel uncomfortable with something, it is better to sort out the initial discomfort and get on with life. Not dealing with a problem can leave you feeling out of control and can result in you erecting barriers or blockages. Start out by talking about the area that is causing discomfort or is becoming a problem, perhaps by a good heart-to-heart with someone known and trusted.

It is also important to seek professional help where appropriate. This should not cause any embarassment, but should be seen as a therapeutic and healthy path to follow. Talking it over with a professional will possibly prevent physical illness. However, therapy should be ongoing; you must work at maintaining your emotional and mental wellbeing. Both individual and group therapy is widely available. Personal development courses can also help. It is your life, so make it as comfortable and happy as possible.

CHAPTER THIRTEEN

Stress

Stress is something that we all suffer from now and again. It usually rears its ugly head during negative times, such as the breakdown of a relationship, yet positive and eagerly awaited events can also give rise to stress. Basically, stress occurs when the pressure of living exceeds your ability to cope with it, because it triggers off changes in your body and you can end up feeling out of control. Stress can be energy draining and in some cases downright exhausting. When suffering from stress you are not free to be your own person.

We all suffer from a certain amount of stress, but too much can be extremely unhealthy and prolonged stress threatens to cause real problems. It leads to poor self-image, negative thinking and eventually attacks your immune systems to bring on physical ailments, such as lack

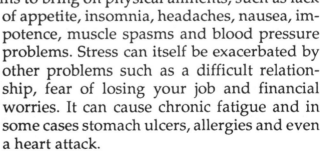

of appetite, insomnia, headaches, nausea, impotence, muscle spasms and blood pressure problems. Stress can itself be exacerbated by other problems such as a difficult relationship, fear of losing your job and financial worries. It can cause chronic fatigue and in some cases stomach ulcers, allergies and even a heart attack.

Yet stress is not always bad. Everyday situations can initiate and create stress responses that motivate us. Therefore, it is your reaction to stress that matters. Reacting stressfully to a stressful situation brings on further stress. It is like being on a merry-go-round with a defunct stop button.

WHERE DOES STRESS COME FROM

You experience stress from three sources — your environment, your thoughts and your body. In each case you are being bombarded with changes demanding that you adjust. In all cases, your security, safety and self esteem are under threat.

Our reactions to these threats can cause bodily changes that are stressful in themselves. Stress begins with your own observation and appraisal of a situation. In other words you must ask yourself what is going on. Trying to recognise the situations that are particularly stressful, whether it be a job, relationship or family. Taking a closer look at where your energy levels are being used can tell you a great deal. Is your energy being used up through

your thought process, emotions or behaviour? The following questions might be thought-provoking.

1. Is my thinking negative or positive?

2. How do I feel about myself?

3. Is there guilt, worry or fear in my life and if so why?

4. Is there a reward for holding onto my stress?

5. How do I talk about myself? What kind of language do I use — negative or positive?

Also, have a look at your expectations, but be realistic in deciding whether or not they can be achieved. In essence you must be able to recognise stress and be equipped to tackle it. Remember it can be a very sly attacker. You may not be fully aware of its presence.

WHAT CAUSES STRESS?

Anything that threatens your ability to cope can bring about stress. Anxiety descends when you are not able to cope with the normal demands of living. It arrives when you allow trivial issues to become major ones. The demands and challenges of life; inner struggles; events; people and places can all create stress. Some people can cope, a few even thrive on stress, believing it gives them an edge, particularly in business. Other people are not so well equipped. They let demands pile up until they're so stressed that they haven't a hope of tackling them. They spend their time re-acting to situations, rather than acting. In effect, they mentally replay problems and often choose to re-act to negative situations, rather than positive ones.

They let other people upset them. They blame others for their problems and often avoid any kind of confrontation. They are likely to be unassertive and bad communicators. They can end up isolating themselves, rather than face people who, kindly or otherwise, will force them to face up to the issues and problems concerning them.

Generally speaking, you assess a situation (either real or imagined) and weigh up whether or not you have the resources to cope with it. You may feel an inability to manage or a fear of not being able to meet a particular demand. You may recognise a demand, but a denial that you cannot meet it can result in total exhaustion, both mental and physical.

REACTING POSITIVELY TO STRESS

If you find yourself in a stressful situation, it is necessary for you to decide to get control back into the area from which it has been lost. The first step is recognising that you are suffering. Your physical and mental health are especially affected. You must learn how to relax.

Here are some guidelines on how to prepare yourself to deal with stress when it occurs.

1. Calm down, breathe deeply — yoga, exercise, etc can help.

2. Look at particular problems and decide which are real and which are imagined.

3. Try to go about tackling these problems and stick with your choice of solution. Also check your progress.

4. Get organised. Disorganisation brings on more stress.

5. Get your body and mind back into shape. Follow a good diet, get ample sleep and regular exercise.

6. Promote a positive self-image. Affirm yourself. Don't be afraid to tell yourself that you are attractive, intelligent and confident.

The old saying that prevention is better than cure is often true. If you are prepared for stress, it cannot sneak up on you so easily. You can prepare yourself for certain times of the day, week and month when you know that added strains and demands could open the door to stress. You should learn — if necessary, by taking a course — to be assertive.

Communicating better with others and generally looking after number one by taking care of your physical, emotional and mental health will increase your resilience. You should have fun and avoid dwelling on past failures and mistakes — it's wasted energy. You can use your energies more positively. Of course everything depends on your attitude. Optimists don't accept failure easily and rarely dwell on past failures.

CHAPTER FOURTEEN

The Balance Sheet

All your resources are related to your energy levels, but you often tend to forget this basic fact. Energy is the source of all your actions, beliefs, feelings and motives. As a child you have boundless energy, but in adult life your energy levels tend to take something of a nose-dive. It is very important that you become aware of how you use your energy, and in order to have a healthy life you must learn how to balance your energy levels. You must aim to rid yourself of wasters of energy and devote the energy saved to the promotion of positive and beneficial thinking and actions.

Anything worthwhile in this life demands effort, which in turn demands that you utilise energy supplies. Effort combined with energy will give effective results. Personal aspirations can be achieved with an effective combination

of effort and energy. Your aim should be to make the effort so enjoyable that it becomes almost effortless.

For example writing this book took a lot of effort, so we had to prepare our energy levels. Initially, we struggled a bit because it was a new experience and we didn't know what amount of energy was required. However, as time went on we developed a rhythm and discovered what degree of energy was required to complete our task. Soon, we began to enjoy the experience and it became almost effortless. Our ally was the knowledge that we would have an end product. We had a goal to work towards and we weren't going to be sidetracked into wasting our energy on trivia.

WHERE DOES ENERGY COME FROM

Energy comes from your physical being. It is necessary, therefore, to nourish the body with foodstuffs. Your home economics classes taught you the value of nutrients, especially protein, while your biology classes dealt with the digestion and utilisation of your food intake. However, energy also comes from how you integrate your thought process and your emotional being with your behavioural patterns which will help your energy levels. When wishing to achieve a certain goal you must decide what effort is required and examine whether you have the energy levels necessary to complete the task. If the effort demanded is too high then you may decide to give up the struggle. On the other hand you may decide that your end goal is obtainable and worth an increase in effort. This increase in effort must be fuelled by an increase in energy levels. Prioritising what you believe to be important is the first step in increasing these levels. You may have to sacrifice another project in order to obtain your end goal.

It is important that you are aware that there are choices available to you. These choices help prevent the misuse of energy. Knowing you have choices can give you the courage to abandon one project in favour of another, more beneficial one.

Here are a few pointers to aid in the choosing of more beneficial paths:

1. Listen to your physical, mental and emotional needs.

2. Get feedback on what you are doing from yourself and others.

3. Listen to what people say, and give their proposals due consideration. Also have your ears open to what is not being said — it can speak volumes!

4. Look for indications that your energy is being depleted through a mis-use of effort:

PHYSICAL PAIN is the most jarring symptom. It signals that you must stop.

STRESS is another. It signals that you have overloaded your system and must take a break.

UNHAPPINESS tells you that the energy and effort being put into your emotional life is not paying dividends.

All the above are destructive operators and changes must be made in order to banish them. You must change paths and travel another that is constructive in terms of your personal growth. In doing so you can reap many benefits. In short, life can become effortless and enjoyment becomes your travelling companion.

However, too often you don't listen to what is going on within you and around you. You spend your time making 'excuses' and refuse to face reality. You use excuses to block out effective action, actions that demanded energy and effort. Eventually, you become exhausted by your own inefficiency. Exhaustion leads to poor concentration, irritability, anxiety, destruction of sleep and eating patterns and very low energy levels. You should avoid casting blame on external forces for your own bad feelings about life. It's worth remembering that nothing outside yourself can control your feelings, thoughts and actions. Becoming friends with yourself, learning to say enough is enough — or, in other words, learning how to exit from a useless and non-productive thought process or emotional wrangle is an important part of coping. Be aware that enemies come in more guises than the human form. Learn to recognise those enemies.

Having unobtainable goals or unreasonable expectation levels is only asking for trouble. If what you have aimed at is unobtainable an unnecessary pressure is created. If you have done everything humanly possible to obtain a goal or resolve a situation and you're still not seeing any results, then you mustn't be afraid to cut your losses and get out — without making any excuses for doing so. Nor should you give in to the temptation to go back and have another shot at it. It will only cause you more pain and will leave you with less energy for more enjoyable tasks. We are all allowed to make mistakes and we can all learn to forgive ourselves.

You should aim to be comfortable wherever you are at any time, age or in any situation and be able to express this comfort in a confident manner. You should exercise your power of choice without being afraid to encounter failure. Pampering yourself should be possible without making excuses for doing so. You should ask yourself what you did well and examine what things you enjoyed and what you didn't. Consider what you're willing to give and what you're willing to receive, in your personal as well as your professional life. You can give yourself a boost by concentrating on what you have rather than what you have not got.

CHAPTER FIFTEEN

A 'Treat-meant' for you

As a child a treat was usually given in recognition of good behaviour or to celebrate a special event, like a birthday.

Sometimes you got treats when you were sick or when you succeeded in the classroom or on the sports-field.

In later life, you go along to the doctor when you need treatment — usually when you are feeling ill or at your worst. Sometimes the feeling of wanting that childhood treat pops-up when things are not going your way or when you feel you ought to be rewarded.

However, in adulthood, treats are an infrequent event. Birthdays, Christmas and illness are likely treat occasions. In between, it's important to be able to give yourself a special treat, especially when no-one else comes forward to spoil you.

HOW TO TREAT YOURSELF

Start by treating yourself with respect. You will soon discover that others will too.

Have a treat programme suitable to your own needs, whether they be daily, weekly or monthly.

You can have an individual treat programme or you can ask family, friends, partners or work colleagues also to enjoy the treat experience.

Your treatment package should include the following:

1. Treats for the physical self, whether it be a visit to the

theatre or a meal out. More serious physical treatments may require a visit to the doctor. Also look at your diet and your exercise programme.

2. Treats for the inner self. Believe that you are a worthwhile individual who takes responsibility for your own enjoyment.

3. Treats for the thinking-self. Learn to sharpen your thinking process by stimulating it with new material.

4. The integrated you. Aim to combine the above three into an overall package by updating your programme at a pace that suits you.

TIPS FOR THAT TREAT-MEANT FOR YOU

1. Don't complicate your life.

2. Get out of the fast lane if feel you can't keep up with the pace. Move at a pace that is comfortable for you.

3. Constantly update your treatment package.

4. Live in reality, not fantasy.

5. Become aware of surroundings and situations that create an atmosphere of comfort and calm — for you.

6. Enjoy yourself.

7. Enjoy the company of others.

8. Maintain your own self-respect and dignity.

9. Have fun.

10. Make the issue a treat-meant for you.

Not *the end*— A begining?